DATE DUE

SEP 5 1981			Good
JUL 2 0 1987			

Poynter, Margaret.
Frisbee fun / by Margaret Poynter ; photographs by Robert S. Poynter. -- New York : Messner, c1977.
96 p. : ill. ; 22 cm.

Frisbee Fun

MOONLIGHTER FRISBEE

MOONLIGHTER FRISBEE

MOONLIGHTER FRISBEE

Frisbee Fun

by MARGARET POYNTER

Photographs by Robert Poynter

JULIAN MESSNER

NEW YORK

 Published by Julian Messner, a Simon & Schuster Division of Gulf & Western Corporations, Simon & Schuster Building, 1230 Avenue of the Americas, New York, New York 10020

Printed in the United States of America
Design by Alex D'Amato

Second Printing, 1977

CREDITS:
Courtesy *FRISBEE WORLD*, P. 10
GARY GOSSETT, PP. 13, 34, 44, 64, 78
ANNE HODGKINSON, P. 9, 26
WILLIAM JABER, P. 19

Library of Congress Cataloging in Publication Data

Poynter, Margaret.
Frisbee fun.

SUMMARY: The history and techniques of playing Frisbee.
1. Frisbee (Game)—Juvenile literature.
[1. Frisbee (Game)] I. Poynter, Robert L.
II. Title.
GV1097.F7P69 796.2 77–23328
ISBN 0–671–32823–9

DEDICATION

To my Frisbee kids—Scott, Bobby, Jennifer, and Joanie
And to Eldon McIntire and Hyper Hank, who turned me
on to the world of Frisbee

ACKNOWLEDGMENTS

I want to thank the many Frisbee-ers who answered my endless questions with so much patience. My special gratitude goes to Jo Cahow and Al Bonopane of the Wham-O Company. Their generous sharing of time and advice made this book possible.

Thanks also to Irv Lander for sharing with me his beautiful philosophy. He exemplifies the spirit of the brotherhood and the sisterhood of Frisbee.

Contents

Unidentified Flying Objects?

Frisbee Beginnings

Darting, sailing, hovering, floating —the sky is filled with flying saucers of blue, red, yellow, green, white. But they aren't *UFO's.* They're very Familiar Flying Objects indeed. They're Frisbees!

Where did Frisbees come from? To go back to the beginning, we'll have to start with Fred Morrison. He was visiting in Bridgeport, Connecticut, one day in 1948. Passing the Frisbie Pie Company, he slowed down to watch two truck drivers throwing empty pie pans back and forth in the parking lot.

A Frisbie pie tin

Fred remembered his childhood in Utah. He and his friends used to throw pie pans—and paint-can lids, and cookie-tin lids.

As he watched, a wind sprang up. The pie pans wobbled and fell to the ground. They were not heavy enough to stay in flight for long.

Fred continued on his way, his inventive mind working on an idea.

When he returned to his home in Los Angeles, Fred went to work. He wanted to make something round and flat, something that would fly through the air even on windy days. He attached a steel ring to the inside rim of a pie pan. This added extra weight.

Fred practiced throwing the pan at a tree trunk. The weight gave the pan enough stability, or steadiness, to sail straight to a target. There was one problem. His invention was heavy enough to fly to the target all right. It was also heavy enough to give someone a good hard knock on the head.

What material would be heavy enough to fly through the air, yet be light enough not to clobber someone who happened to get in the way?

The answer was not long in coming. Plastics were just beginning to be widely used in the late 1940s. Fred studied and read and tested. He found that a simple plastic circle didn't work. But the right design might do it.

Fred worked out the design—a disc, round and flat on bottom, but with a sloped top. Then he curved the rim under, and put small rounded projections on the top of the disc. Finally he had a toy that would fly and that would not harm people who wandered into its flight path. He used a plastic which was soft and resilient, or "bouncy." The disc made with this plastic held up under everything Fred did to it.

He named the disc "Morrison's Flyin' Saucer." Now he had to try to sell it! He tried to think of a "gimmick" to catch people's attention.

He came up with a good one. Fred and a friend went to the County Fair in Pomona, near Los Angeles. They each had a carton of the Flyin' Saucers. They also had something else—bundles of "invisible wire!" Of course, there wasn't any wire. The boxes were empty.

"Make way! Make way for the invisible wire!" Fred called as he made his way through the crowd.

"Invisible wire." "What is he talking about?" "Is he crazy?" Fred heard the people murmuring to each other as he set up two posts several yards apart. He looked very serious as he strung his "wire" between the posts.

The audience quieted down as Fred stood at one post and his friend stood at the other.

"Now I shall throw my flyin' saucer along the length of the wire right into my partner's hand," Fred announced.

Sure enough, the saucer sailed straight as an arrow to his friend's outstretched hand. Over and over again Fred threw the saucer. Not once did it wobble or fall to the ground.

"It sure looks as if that disc is attached to something," said a man. "How much is that wire?"

"One cent a foot," answered Fred. "And I'll give you my Flyin' Saucer free with every hundred feet of wire that you buy."

Every day of the Fair, Fred and his partner did a lot of "invisible wire" business!

After the County Fair closed, Fred decided to improve the design of his Flyin' Saucer. He had noticed that it sailed well when twirled in one direction, but did not work as well in the reverse direction. The projections on the top caused the problem. Off came the projections and Fred had a new toy—the Pluto Platter.

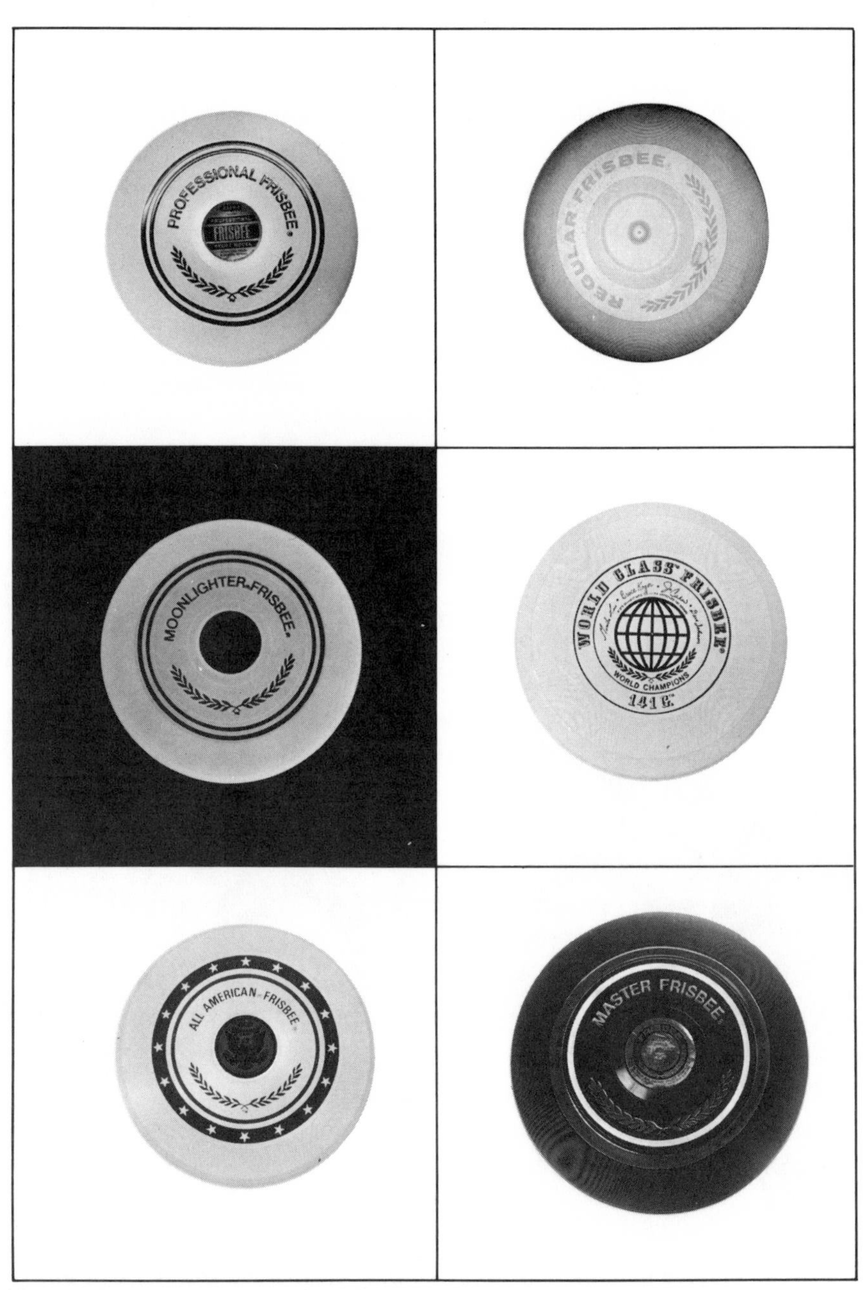

Some of the many models of Frisbees

One day Fred was demonstrating his toy in Los Angeles. Rich Knerr and "Spud" Melin from the Wham-O Company were watching. They liked what

Frisbee players in Japan. In front are U.S. champions Monika Lou and Vic Malafronte

they saw and asked Fred to come out to their factory in San Gabriel, California, to talk about manufacturing more Pluto Platters. Within two years Pluto Platters were being sold in many parts of the United States.

On a visit to Harvard University in Cambridge, Massachusetts, Rich Knerr was pleased to see some students throwing Pluto Platters. They told him how they used to throw Frisbie Company pie tins. In fact, "Frisbie-ing" was what they were calling their Pluto Platter games.

Rich remembered Fred Morrison telling him about the Frisbie Pie Company. When he returned to San Gabriel, he talked to Fred and the people at Wham-O. Everyone agreed that it was a great name for their flying disc—but changed the spelling to "Frisbee."

And Frisbee it has been since. Many models have been developed, including a Moonlighter Frisbee which glows in the dark, and a Professional Model.

Frisbee's popularity grew rapidly. Exhibitions by experts, tournaments, and the International Frisbee Association (IFA), helped make it the exciting sport it is today.

Now the Frisbee is soaring outside the borders of the United States. Russian cosmonauts and Chinese ping-pong champions have played catch with the Frisbee. Peace Corps members have taught people in South America and Africa how to play Frisbee. Two United States college students went to the People's Republic of China with their Frisbees, delighting audiences there. And astronauts tossed a plastic disc around on the moon!

Frisbee is played by 30,000,000 people in twenty-eight different countries. And you are one of them.

Maybe you will spend a lot of time playing Frisbee by yourself. Target practice is always a good way to pass the time. Or how about forming a Frisbee team? A little competition can make a game exciting. Or what about the Rose Bowl World Frisbee Championships? Would you like to play Frisbee with 20,000 people cheering you on?

Play Frisbee any way you want. Fun and good exercise are in your hands!

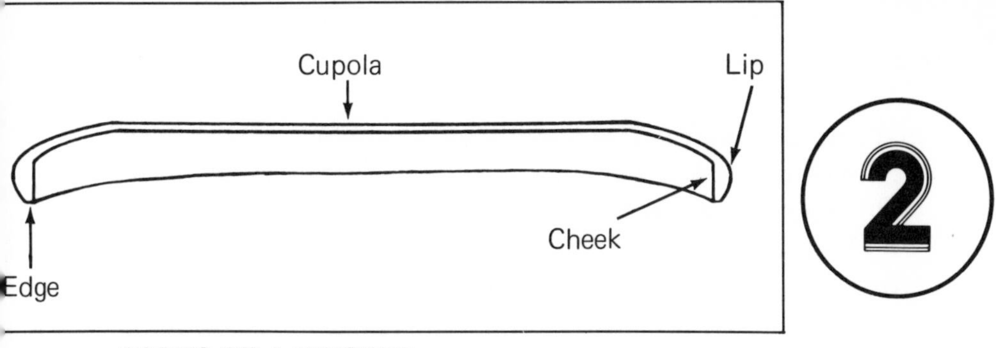

PARTS OF A FRISBEE

2

Frisbee Science

When Fred Morrison made the first Pluto Platter, he didn't think of it as anything but a toy. Little did he dream that his toy would end up being studied by universities, or that it would almost become a part of the United States Navy!

John Kirkland tested his Frisbee out in the wind tunnel at his school, Massachusetts Institute of Technology. He wanted to find ways to improve his throws. Interested professors found that Frisbees were useful in teaching about air pressure, gravity, and winds. Soon other schools borrowed the idea.

Then, in 1968, scientists in the United States Navy started doing tests with the Frisbee. They were looking for a way to keep flares up in the air. Flares are used to light up targets at night. They are usually fired from the ground high into the air, or dropped from airplanes. The slower they fall, the longer their light will last and be useful. The Navy was attaching parachutes to flares to slow them down. The chutes worked fairly well, but they were bulky and hard to handle.

Frisbees are light, steady in flight, and easy to store. The Navy thought Frisbees might be just the thing for keeping flares in the air. For several months they tested Frisbees in wind tunnels, in which air is blown to see the effects of wind pressure. They also threw Frisbees off mountains!

They finally had to admit failure, however. The Frisbee could not overcome both the pull of *gravity,* the force which draws things to the ground, and the weight of the flare.

FRISBEE FLIGHT FACTS

The Navy may not have had much luck with Frisbee flight, but that shouldn't stop you from learning about it. The more you understand about a Frisbee in flight, the better player you will be.

What makes a Frisbee fly? If the answer had to be given in only one word, that word would be air. If you threw the Frisbee into a *vacuum,* a space without air, it would fall to the ground within a few feet.

You can see how air works on a Frisbee by using a tub full of water and any kind of plastic lid. Hold the lid firmly and push it swiftly through the water, tilted slightly. As you push the water down on one end, the water pushes the lid up on the other. Feel this force, or pressure, by placing your fingertips gently on the lid. See how the water bunches up along the forward edge, before it goes on to flow smoothly and quickly over the top.

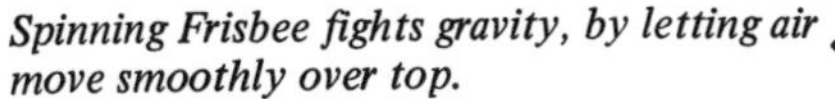

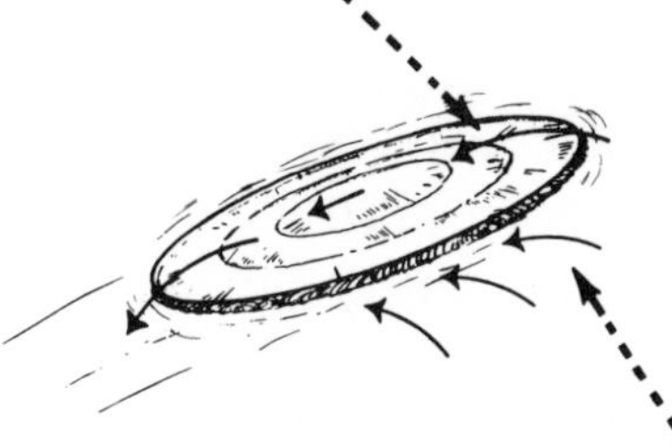

HOW A FRISBEE FLIES

The same things happen to your Frisbee in flight. As the disc leaves your hand, you give it *velocity* (direction and speed) and *spin* (twist). As the Frisbee moves forward, it pushes the air down, and the resulting pressure gives it the lift it needs to fight the pull of gravity. The air flows smoothly over the top of the disc, so there is hardly any air pressure on that side to push the Frisbee down.

Why doesn't all that pressure on the bottom of the Frisbee cause it to flip over backward? Because the *spin* you give the Frisbee when you snap it from your hand enables it to resist. The faster the spin, the more *stability* (steadiness) the Frisbee will have, and the better lift it will gain.

To understand this better, think of a top. The faster a top spins, the better it resists gravity, and so it balances better. In the same way, a fast-spinning Frisbee fights the pull of gravity and the push of air pressure beneath it.

But a Frisbee can't stay up forever. As it flies, the air is bunching up around the leading edge and slowing it. As the Frisbee slows and the spin lessens, gravity starts pulling it back to earth. Even then, if it has gained enough lift, it will settle slowly, like a parachute, fighting gravity all the way down.

The balance, or *ratio,* between all of these things —spin, velocity, air pressure, lift, and gravity—are what determines how far and how long the Frisbee will stay in the air. You can make these things work in your favor by learning how to throw correctly. Smoothness, the swing of your arm, the curling and uncurling of your wrist, and getting the Frisbee into the air at the proper angle, are more important than strength.

A Frisbee is not like a football, which has to be constantly pushed, kicked, and shoved into motion. A Frisbee works with you and the air to stay aloft until the last possible second.

FRISBEE AND THE WEATHER

If you want to get longer flights or do boomerangs, you can make it easier on yourself by paying attention to the wind and weather conditions.

The best time to play Frisbee is when there is little or no wind. Gusts, updrafts, and downdrafts can do things to the disc that you never planned on when you threw it.

Those things aren't always bad, however. A sudden updraft can raise your Frisbee higher than you had dared to hope. A gust of wind hitting the side of your Frisbee in the direction of the spin sometimes helps to carry the disc several yards further than it would have gone otherwise. But a downdraft can cut short a flight that might have set a record. An eddy, or small wind current which is going in the opposite direction to the main wind current, can slow the Frisbee and make it fall short. A Frisbee thrown in the

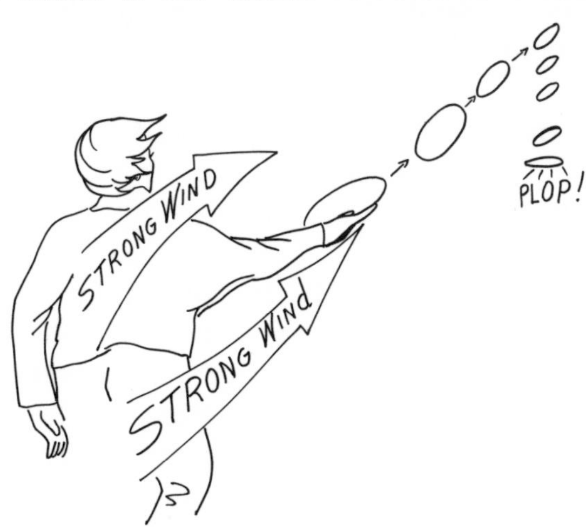

same direction as a strong wind is very likely to *tail-skate* (dive toward the ground), because the pressure on its back will stop the trailing edge from rising.

So, if you play Frisbee in the wind, prepare for the unexpected. However, there are some ways that you can get the wind working in your favor.

You might get lucky and get some good distance flights if there is a strong, steady wind blowing. Stand with your back toward it and try a backhand or an underhand. If the Frisbee doesn't tailskate, you should have a good flight.

You can avoid some wind *turbulence*—sudden changes—by carefully picking the time and place of your Frisbee playing. Don't play in the middle of a warm sunny day, when there is a lot of heat exchanged between the ground and the air. This exchange causes more air movement, or wind. Play on a smooth surface, such as a closely mowed lawn, blacktop, or cement. Air moves more smoothly over a surface when it doesn't have to go around and over things.

A cloudy day could be a good Frisbee day. The air is a little damp, and so lighter than dry air. Your Frisbee will be able to slide through it faster and easier.

If you go to the beach, be sure to take your Frisbee along. The wind at the beach is usually a dependable, steady, onshore breeze. Remember, try to get there early in the day, because that's when the wind should be the lightest. It will probably grow stronger as the day progresses, and will start dying down in the late afternoon. Play at the water's edge, where there is less wind turbulence. You will have better throws and also will not be kicking sand into someone's potato salad! Your Frisbee will float, so you don't have to worry about losing it.

Any weather can be Frisbee weather if you want it to be. One of the fun things about Frisbee-throwing is watching its flight under many different conditions. It can be full of surprises!

Scott McGlasson

Caring-For You and Your Frisbee

Scott McGlasson, a twelve-year-old Frisbee champion, wishes that everyone could learn how to play Frisbee. "Frisbee is a different kind of thing," he says. "There is hardly any chance of anyone getting hurt, like there is in baseball or football."

Frisbee *is* safe. There have been no reports of anyone being badly hurt by a Frisbee. But it is still up to you to follow the safety rules.

World champion Vic Malafronte says, "When playing Frisbee with friends, don't do silly things to prove you have guts. Also, don't lose your temper, or try to be a hero."

When you play Frisbee, choose an open space—a park, a playground, or a big back yard. As you run, *watch where you're going.* You can't blame a flying saucer if you bump into a tree. And throw carefully. Getting back a Frisbee from the top of a tree or from over a high fence can be dangerous!

It is a good idea to get "warmed up" before you start your Frisbee games. When you start out slowly, you are much less likely to end up with shoulder sprains and sore muscles. And smo-o-o-th is the word to think of when you are throwing the Frisbee. That will save wear and tear on your wrist and elbow, and will also make you a better player. Be sure to rest when you get tired. You can always catch better after you've caught your breath.

Cut your fingernails short if you play a lot of Frisbee. Otherwise, you might catch your nails on the edge of the rim. A torn fingernail is not serious, but it hurts.

Bruises? Yes, the Frisbee can give you a black and blue mark if it hits you hard enough. However, it is nothing compared to being struck by a baseball or even a tennis ball. In fact, a ping-pong ball is about the only kind of ball that could hurt you less than a Frisbee.

Use your common sense, relax, and enjoy yourself.

Fly High with

TIPS ON FRISBEE CARE

1. Soap and water are your Frisbee's best friend. Scrub it when needed, using water which is comfortable to your hands—not too hot.
2. Don't leave your Frisbee lying for too long in direct sunlight, especially in a closed car. Too much heat bleaches the Frisbee and can make it lose its shape.
3. Be careful where you throw your Frisbee. If you do certain shots on a rough, hard surface, the Frisbee will get scuffed. Tiny strands of plastic may appear on the edge. You can try steel wool to rub these off—gently.
4. Put your name and address on the underside of your Frisbee, using a broad felt tip pen in a color that will show up.
5. If your Frisbee becomes torn or cracked, there is not much that can be done. Glues and cements and tapes may help for a while, but almost any repair is only temporary. A repaired Frisbee probably won't fly as far, and you might not be able to control it as well.

Vic Malafronte showing his championship form

Grips and Throws

How many ways are there to hold and throw a Frisbee? Just as many as you can make up.

But if you want to become a really good player, there are certain grips and throws that you should learn. The important ones are described in this chapter. If you are just learning Frisbee, try them and pick out the one that feels best for the way *you* want to play.

GRIPS

A "grip" is a special way of holding the Frisbee. There are four important grips.

1. The Common Grip

Put your thumb on top of the Frisbee. Stretch your first finger out along the *lip* (the outer rim). Put the rest of your fingers under the Frisbee. For a strong, sure grip push against the edge of the Frisbee with the tip of your first finger.

2. The Thumb Grip

Put your thumb underneath the lip. Press it hard against the *cheek* (inner surface of the rim) of the Frisbee. Put your fingers on top.

3. The Two-Finger or Sidearm Grip

Put your thumb on top of the Frisbee. Put your first and second fingers underneath. Just leave your last two fingers loose, or curl them back against your palm.

4. Wrist Flip

This grip is good to use when you are throwing from a small space.

Put your thumb close to the cheek of the Frisbee. Stretch your first finger out along the lip. Spread your other fingers out on top.

Practice these grips until you find one or two that feel just right for *your* hand.

THE TARGET

Make a target by drawing a circle about twelve feet across on the ground. You can use chalk on pavement, or you can form one from rocks on the dirt or grass.

Have a friend stand inside the circle and catch the Frisbee. Throw from 25 feet away. You should throw so that your friend does not have to step outside the lines of the circle to make the catch.

An upright Frisbee target is made of a circle three feet across. It is hung about three feet off the ground between two posts. The target can be an old Hula Hoop, or a piece of heavy cardboard with a circle cut out. Your throw is good if it passes through the circle, even if it touches the inside edge.

If you are just starting to throw for accuracy, stand about ten feet away from the upright target. Then as you find it easier to hit the target, move further back. Try fifteen yards and then finally go to twenty.

If you can hit the target over and over again from a distance of twenty yards, *then* you can think of yourself as a skilled Frisbee thrower!

THROWS

Sight your target before you throw by stretching your arm out, Frisbee in hand, pointing at the target.

Put your whole body into your throw. Your feet should be set about as far apart as the width of your shoulders. Your arms and legs should feel loose and "springy." Use your free arm to balance yourself as you throw. Sometimes you will want to use *follow-through,* letting your arm finish its swing after the Frisbee has left your hand.

Sighting the target

Following through—with all his might!

Here are four throws that you will use often.

1. The Backhand

The backhand is good for both distance and accuracy.

- Use the common grip. Stand with your throwing side toward the target.
- Sight your target. Then smoothly bring your arm across your body, *curling* your wrist during the swing. Tilt the Frisbee toward you during the curling. Immediately bring your arm forward again, *uncurling* your wrist as you do.

Preparing to make a backhand throw

Follow the arm positions from right to left for
CURLING

Follow the arm positions from left to right for
UNCURLING

- At the point of release, *uncock* your wrist—bend it back with a snap—and point your first finger at the target. This puts spin on the Frisbee so it can fly.

Got it? It's forward, back, forward, snap! One smooth motion.

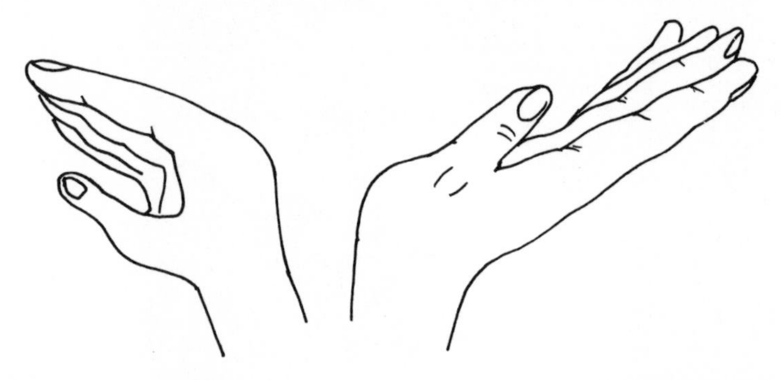

COCKING THE WRIST **UNCOCKING**

If you are throwing for distance, you will want as much *arc*—curve—as you can get. To do this, after you stretch your arm toward the target in Step 2, bring it out and back from your throwing side. Then go ahead and bring it across your body.

2. The Underhand

- Use the common grip. Face the target. Sight it.
- Swing your arm down and back, as if you were throwing a bowling ball. Smoothly bring your arm forward again. At the same time take one step forward, using your right foot if you are throwing with your left hand, and your left foot if you are throwing with your right hand.

- At the point of release, uncock your wrist, and point your first finger at the target.
- If you are trying for distance, curl your wrist as you bring your arm back. Uncurl it on the forward swing.

There you go. Forward, back, forward, snap! Smo-o-o-o-th.

3. The Curve

With this throw, the Frisbee curves in the air after it leaves your hand. It will approach the target from the side.

- Curves may be thrown many ways, but it is easiest to start with the backhand.
- *Tilt* the Frisbee to the left for a left curve, to the right for a right curve. The more the Frisbee is tilted the more it will curve. Keep the same amount of tilt during the backward-forward swing.
- If you are trying for accuracy, aim to the right of the target in a right curve throw. Aim to the left of the target in a left curve throw.

4. Skipshot

In a skipshot, the edge of the Frisbee hits the ground *once,* about halfway to the target, before being caught. For this throw you should be playing on a hard surface, or very short grass.

- Use the backhand throw. If you have a very good underhand throw you can also use that.
- Tilt the Frisbee to the left. Aim toward the ground.

Problems?

Does the Frisbee hit the ground too soon? You have probably aimed too low. Does it bounce around instead of just hitting the ground once? You may have tilted the Frisbee too much. Does it hit the ground upside down? You probably tilted it to the right. Does it land flat? You forgot to tilt it at all.

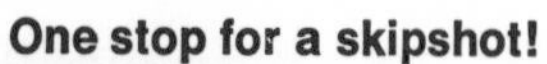

One stop for a skipshot!

TIPS

Throwing for accuracy

1. You do not have to use follow-through.
2. Keep your eye on the target during the entire throw.
3. Position your body correctly.
4. Use backhand or underhand throw.
5. At the point of release, point your first finger at the target.

Throwing for distance

1. Follow-through is important.
2. Take a running start before you throw.
3. The more curl you have, the further the Frisbee will go.
   Curl your wrist as you bring your arm back. The Frisbee should be tilted toward your body.
4. Uncurl your wrist completely as you bring your arm forward.
5. The more arc, the more distance you will get.
6. Study the chapter on Frisbee Science. If you learn about air currents and pay attention to them, you will be able to get longer flights.

Problems?

Does the Frisbee turn over in flight when you are using either the backhand or the underhand?

You may have released the Frisbee too flat. Don't forget your slight upward tilt.

Does your Frisbee wobble in flight?

Make sure your uncurling is smooth and you have a good wrist snap.

Peter Bloeme, champion, prepares a tricky throw

Trick Throws

If you have become good at doing some of the important throws, maybe you would like to practice some trick ones. Then you can start amazing your friends with your Frisbee-ing!

1. The Sidearm Throw

Want a speedy flight? Then this throw is the one for you.

- Use the two-finger grip. Bend your elbow and hold your throwing arm out from your side.

- Now bring your arm back. Uncurl your wrist as far as you can as your arm moves back.
- Bring your arm forward until it is just in front of your throwing side.
- Quickly uncock your wrist at the point of release. The Frisbee should "pop" out of your hand.

Got the idea? Arm bent and out, back, forward, snap! —one continuous motion.

You might find it helpful to practice step 4 over and over again without actually throwing the Frisbee. As you practice, hold your throwing arm with your free hand, so your throwing arm won't move. In other words, you will have the feel of the Frisbee "popping" out of your hand.

Sidearm throw

2. Ground Throw or Roller

In this one, the Frisbee will roll in a straight line along the ground.

- Use the two–finger grip.
- Stand facing the target. Bend your elbow and bring the Frisbee straight up to the side of your head.

- Bring your arm back, then forward.
- Aim toward the ground. Release the Frisbee as your arm comes down. Uncock your wrist at the point of release.
- You can also throw a roller from a kneeling position. Throw a backhand and aim toward the ground.

Getting ready to make a thumb flip

3. The Thumber or Thumb Flip

This throw dips and moves sideways in the air, making it very hard to catch. It's not a very good shot to use for accuracy. Use it when you want a speedy flight.

- Use the thumb grip. Bend your elbow and cock it.
- Bend your wrist until the Frisbee is touching your arm.

- Swing your arm back, keeping your elbow cocked.
- Bring your arm forward and uncock your wrist at the point of release.
- Stiffen the elbow, back, forward, snap! Now watch someone try to catch *that* one.

4. Hover Flight or Floater

There should be a little wind for this one. The Frisbee will have a beautiful flight—a high climb and a slow fall. It settles toward the ground almost like a parachute, giving the catcher plenty of time to make trick catches.

- Use a backhand throw.
- Stand facing the wind. Aim forward and slightly up.
- Throw smoothly and easily.

5. The Boomerang

Want to catch your own throws? You can with the boomerang. If you do it right, the Frisbee will sail up, out, then back to you. The boomerang is actually a hover, only more so.

Stand facing the wind.

Tilt the leading edge of the Frisbee up slightly. Aim forward and up. (Don't confuse aiming with tilting. Tilting is done with the hand. Aiming is done with the arm.)

The wind will slow the flight and send the Frisbee back to you.

FLIGHT PATH OF A BOOMERANG THROW

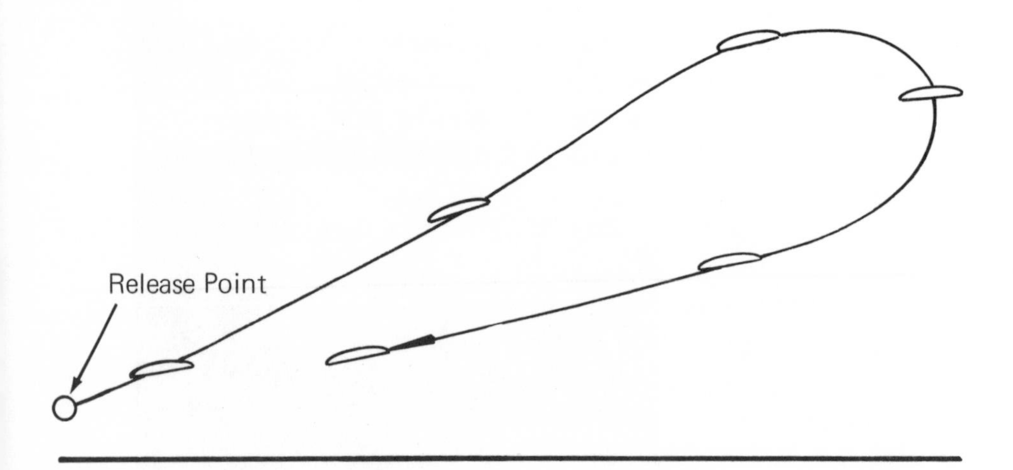

Catches

You know, of course, that you can catch a Frisbee with your hands. But you may also want to catch it with one finger. How about between your knees? And don't forget your feet.

There are many ways to catch a Frisbee. Here again, you can make up your own special catches, or you can pick one of the catches in this chapter.

No matter how you catch the Frisbee, there are some things to remember. First, a good catch begins down in your toes! Stand with your feet apart about as far as the width of your shoulders. Then put your weight on the balls (the front part) of your feet. That way you'll be ready to move quickly in any direction. Keep your knees bent a little. They should feel "springy"—loose and raring to go. Your arms should feel loose, too. Shake them to get the kinks out.

• Keep your eyes on the Frisbee as it comes toward you. When it is about halfway between you and the thrower, start turning toward it. Unless it is coming low and fast, you won't have to hurry. The Frisbee slows a lot during the last third of its flight, so you will have plenty of time to prepare for the catch.

• If you want to throw the Frisbee back right away, catch it with your throwing hand. If there is no hurry about returning it, catch it with your other hand. It is a good idea to be able to use both hands almost equally well.

A good catch!

Now here are some catches for you to practice.

1. One-Handed Catch

Hold your hand loosely, with your fingers bent a little. The rim of the Frisbee should land in the space or "pocket" between your thumb and first finger.

• Is the Frisbee coming toward you *above* your waist? Then turn your palm down. This is called "thumbs down." If the Frisbee is approaching *below* your waist, then catch it with your palm up. This is "thumbs up."

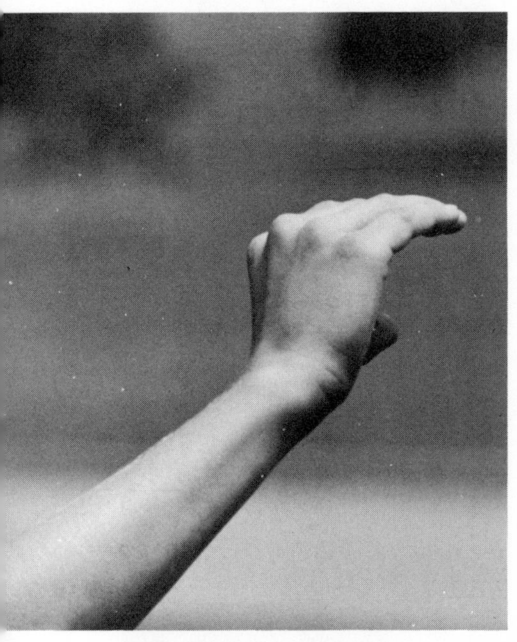

Palm down for a thumbs down catch. . . .

. . . .and palm up for a thumbs up catch

2. Behind-the-Back Catch

The Frisbee should be approaching at about waist level.

• Face the Frisbee. For a right-hand catch, twist your body to the right. Your left side is facing the thrower. Reach your right hand behind your back, and catch the Frisbee as it passes your left side. For a left-hand catch twist to the left, and catch the Frisbee as it passes your right side.

3. Between-the-Legs Catch

Use this catch for low throws or skip shots.

• Face the Frisbee. As it approaches, move so that it will pass between your legs.

• Reach behind and through your legs to make the catch.

4. Trailing-Edge Catch

Use this catch if the Frisbee is approaching over head level.

• Face the Frisbee. Let the leading edge—the side closest to you—pass over your head. Then catch onto the trailing edge with all four fingers.

• To make a **one-finger trailing-edge catch,** stretch out your first finger under the Frisbee and "snag" or catch it by the rim. Slow it down by turning your hand around and around slowly in the same direction that the Frisbee is spinning.

• For a **between-the-legs, trailing-edge catch,** let the Frisbee pass between your legs and catch it by the trailing edge.

One-finger catch

An upside down between-the-legs catch!

She's got it! A trailing-edge catch

5. Blind Catch

This catch is impressive, but it is not hard to do. The Frisbee should be coming straight toward you and should be above waist level.

• Bend forward from your waist and stretch both arms behind your back and up.

• Let the Frisbee sail over your head and into your hands.

6. Tipping

Tipping is not really a catch. It is more a way of keeping the Frisbee in the air longer. It gives you extra time to get ready to make a trick catch.

• The Frisbee should be approaching slowly at head level or above. Hold all of your fingers together and straight up. Hit the underside of the Frisbee as close

to the center as possible. Keep hitting it as long as you want it to stay in the air.

• If you do much finger tipping, you should wear a plastic thimble on the finger you use the most.

• You can also tip with your foot if the Frisbee is approaching low enough. Strike it gently on the underside with your toes. Then make the catch with your hand.

7. Nail Delay

This is a variation of tipping. If you bite your nails, this is not for you!

• If the Frisbee is approaching above eye level, hold your hand with the palm facing away from you. If the Frisbee is below eye level, your palm should be facing toward you.

• Slightly bend your index or your middle finger as the Frisbee comes down. It will land on your fingernail. The Frisbee will keep spinning rapidly as long as your nail is in contact with it.

When you can make several catches and throws easily, start using your body more. In Frisbee playing, half the fun is jumping, twisting, bending, turning and running. Try a behind-the-back catch while jumping off the ground, twisting all the way around, and throwing the Frisbee back, all in one nonstop motion.

Use a trailing-edge catch, but don't catch it until the Frisbee has passed way over your head. Lean backward as far as you can to make the catch. Then you can quickly come forward and make a fast underhand throw.

Try tipping with your elbow or your head!

Develop your own routine and become a free-style champ.

Jo Cahow, a world Frisbee champion, says "Practice is the important thing. Every time you throw or catch, you are getting a little bit better.

"Actually, Frisbee-ing is 50 percent self-confidence. The other 50 percent is practice and experience."

Vic Malafronte agrees with her. "Only with practice can you be consistent," he says. "And it's consistency, not muscles or power, that makes champions."

Jo Cahow

Games and Contests

As you play Frisbee, you might easily think up some of your own special games. But just to get you started, here are a few that you can try.

GAMES

Catch

All you need for this game is one Frisbee and a friend or two. Try all the throws and catches that you know. Practice some new ones.

Airbrushing

Is there a wind? Then try some airbrushing.

• Face the wind. Toss the Frisbee a foot or two into the air and immediately start hitting the trailing edge with the palm of your hand. Keep pushing the Frisbee into the wind.

• When you become expert at airbrushing, you will be able to keep the Frisbee in the air as long as the wind holds out.

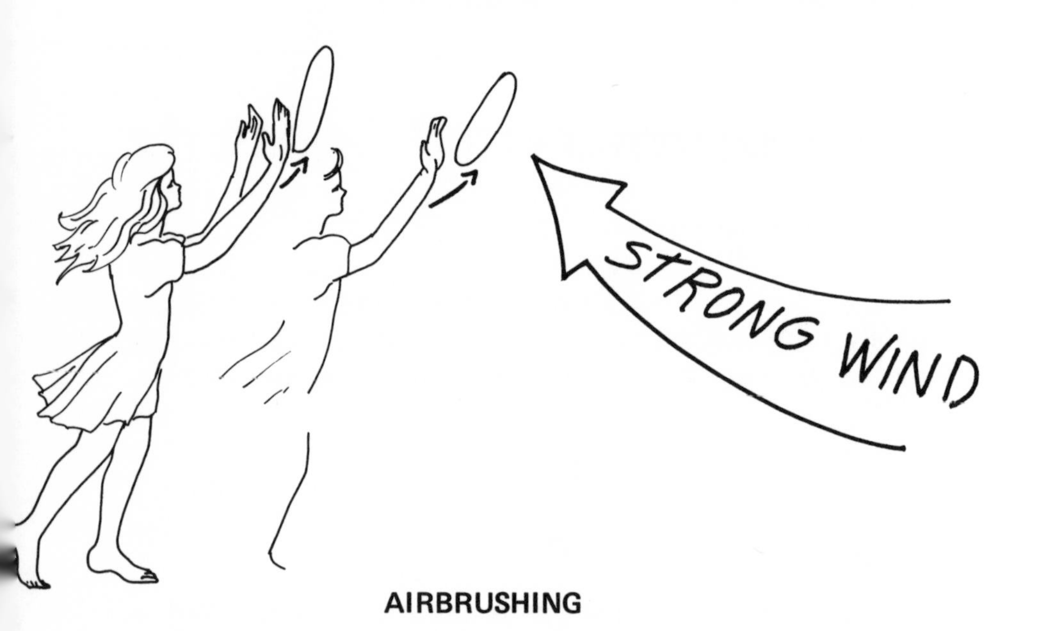

AIRBRUSHING

Follow the Leader

For this game you need one Frisbee and a friend who is just about as good at Frisbee as you are.

• To start the game, throw the Frisbee any way you choose. If you use a backhand, then your friend must use the backhand to throw the Frisbee back to you.

• But you are not going to have it all your way. *You* must use the same catch that your friend used. Was it a behind-the-back? Then you must use the behind-the-back.

There you go—it's follow the leader, but with a difference. There are *two* leaders in this game.

Sweet Georgia Brown

"Sweet Georgia Brown" is the favorite song of the Harlem Globetrotters in their fun basketball exhibitions.

• For Frisbee Sweet Georgia Brown, you need one Frisbee and from four to ten players. Everyone stands in a circle about fifteen or twenty feet apart. The idea is to keep the Frisbee going around and around the circle just as fast as you can. The players can use any throw or catch they want.

• Keep your eye on the Frisbee. It usually gets back to you faster than you think it will.

Keepaway

You need one Frisbee and three or more players.

• Pick one player to be "it." The other players throw and catch the Frisbee as fast as they can. No fair holding onto it for more than a second.

The idea is to keep the Frisbee away from "it." What if "it" manages to catch it? Then the one who threw the Frisbee last takes "its" place.

Obstacle Course

You usually play Frisbee in an open space. But here is one game where you need trees, bushes, small sheds, or telephone poles. You also need three or four players, each with a Frisbee.

• Before you start to play, get together and map out a course. You need eight or ten "obstacles" or "hurdles" along the course. The Frisbee must be thrown—not carried—over, around, through, or under the obstacles.

• The player who gets to the end of the course with the least number of throws is the winner.

CONTESTS

What is the difference between a game and a contest? Usually you can play a game anytime. A contest should be planned out ahead of time. And sometimes a contest will include more than one game. Are there quite a few Frisbee players in your school? How about some of you getting together and talking to the person in charge of the playground about organizing a Frisbee contest?

In a contest it's a good idea to have the players no more than a year or two apart in age. Then the competition is more fair, and there is less chance of a younger person being hurt.

You will need to choose a date, a time, and a place for the contest. You will need a judge, who must know the rules, and should be older than the players. Then pick out the games you want to have.

You might want to have prizes for the winners. Maybe everyone could put in 25 cents to buy a new Frisbee for a grand prize. You could have someone who prints or writes very well make up certificates to give to the best players.

Bullseye

You need a target and five Frisbees for this game. The target is like a large dartboard laid out on the ground. (See the illustration.) You can use chalk, rope, or medium-sized rocks to mark out the circles and numbers.

• The idea is for the players to get as many points as they can by throwing the Frisbee into the smaller circles.

• All of the players line up at the throwing line. The judge stands near the target with paper and pencil to keep score. Each player throws the five Frisbees one after the other. He or she must not step beyond the throwing line.

• The Frisbee must land all the way inside of the circle to count for that circle. If it lands on the line between two circles, the points for the larger circle are counted.

• Each player's points are added up by the judge. When all players have thrown, the one with the highest score is the winner.

If two or more players make the same score, those players will play again until there is a winner.

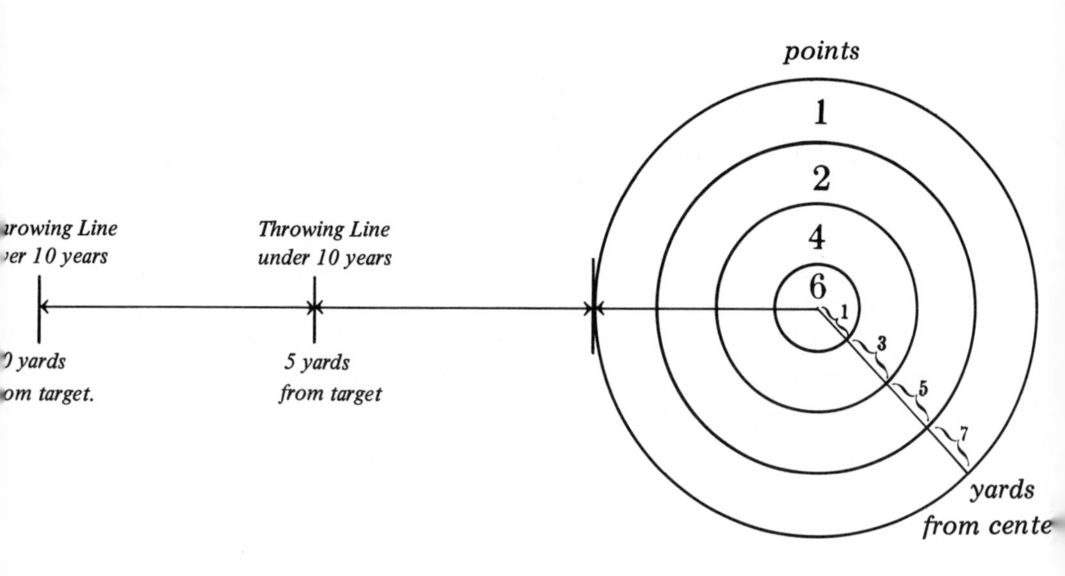

LAYOUT FOR BULLSEYE

Distance Accuracy

You need five Frisbees, a marked off throwing area, and a tape measure.

Rocks with distances in yards painted on them are laid out in a straight line from a throwing line (see diagram).

The idea is for the players to throw as straight and as far as they can.

• The players line up at the throwing line. The judge stands at the far end of the distance line. Each player throws all five Frisbees one after the other.

• The best throw out of the five is the one which counts. To score, the judge marks down how far the Frisbee went along the distance line before it landed. Then the judge measures how far to the side of the distance line the Frisbee landed. This number is subtracted from the first number. The result will be the final or "net" score.

For instance, if the Frisbee goes 25 yards along the distance line, and it lands five yards to the side of that line, the "net" score is 20 yards.

The player with the highest net score wins.

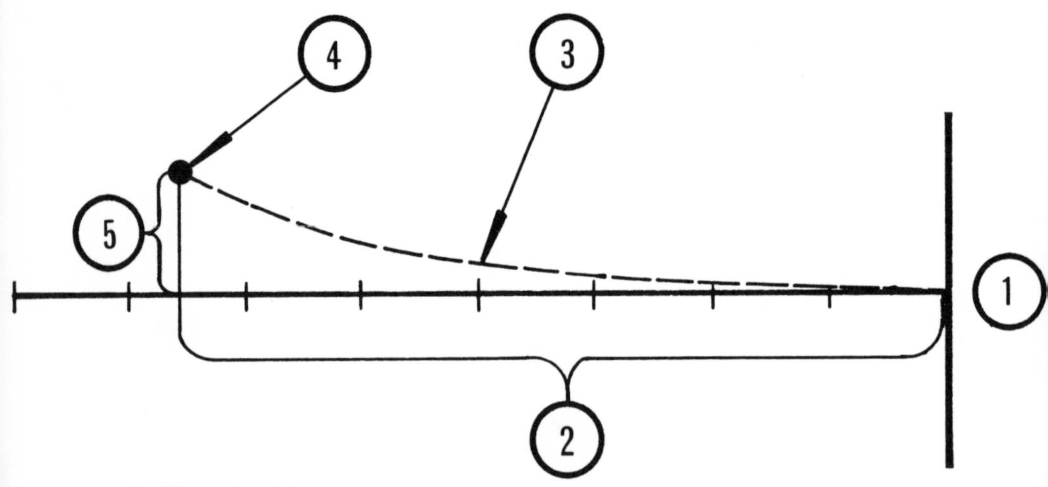

1. *Throwing Line*
2. *Distance line marked off in yards*
3. *Flight path*
4. *Landing Point*
5. *Off-side measurement*

LAYOUT FOR DISTANCE ACCURACY

Discathon

This event is something like the obstacle course game.

• You need one Frisbee for each player and a course which has been marked out ahead of time. Each Frisbee must have the player's name on it so there won't be any mix-ups.

• The course can be anywhere from one-fourth to one mile long, depending on how much space you have, and how much time you want to spend on this game. Trees, water fountains, poles, small sheds, or bushes can be used as obstacles. Mark each obstacle plainly with bright-colored tape, ribbon or chalk. If necessary, give each player a small hand-drawn map of the course. It is important that everyone knows the layout and where the ending is.

• The player who gets to the end of the course first, wins. The Frisbee must be picked up and thrown from whatever spot it lands on. There should be at least two judges—three if there are many players, and the course is a long one. Two of the judges travel along with the players. The third waits at the end of the course to declare the winner.

There are some **do-nots** in this game:

1. Do not throw anyone else's Frisbee.
2. Do not get in the way of anyone else's Frisbee.
3. Do not take short cuts. Every player must travel along the whole course.

DISCATHON COURSE

4. Do not carry the Frisbee. It must be thrown along the whole course. If it lands off the course, the player must throw it from where it landed.

5. Do not be in such a hurry that you forget to watch where you're going. Good throwing will get you to the end of the course sooner than fast running will.

Marathon

For this game you need five to eight teams, with two players on each team. Each team must have one Frisbee. There should be one judge. The judge needs a watch with a second hand.

• Mark off two parallel lines on the ground. If most of the players are beginners with the Frisbee, the lines should be ten yards apart. They can be fifteen yards apart for better players. The two members of each team face each other along the lines. The teams should be about five yards apart. Throws and catches must be made behind the lines.

• Before the game starts, the players can spend two or three minutes throwing their Frisbees around to get warmed up. The judge will tell everyone when warm-up time is over.

• When the game begins, the judge will start to count, calling out one number every ten seconds. Each time the judge calls out a number, one team member must throw to his or her partner.

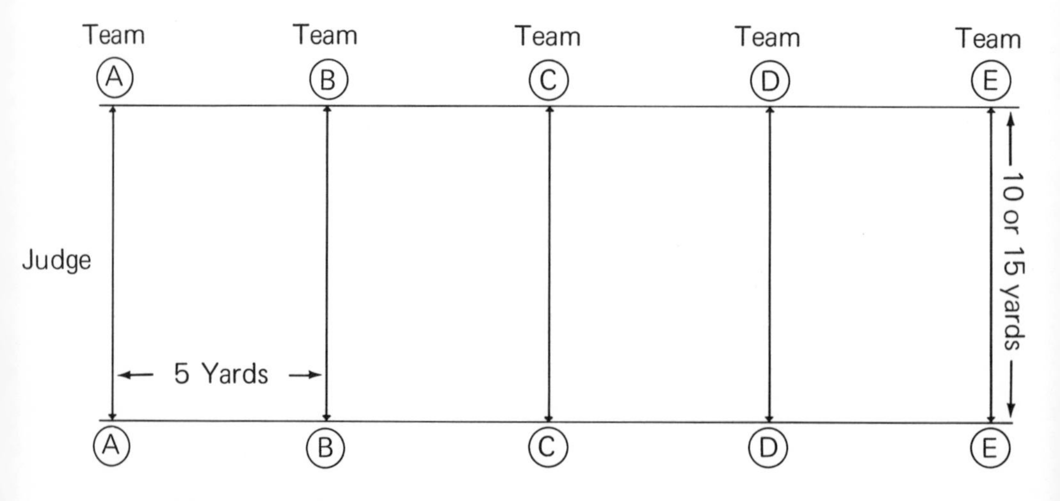

LAYOUT FOR MARATHON

• If the catcher does not make the catch from behind the line, or if the Frisbee is dropped, that team is out of the game.

• The game keeps on until there is only one team left: the winner!

Speedflow

The idea here is for a team of two players to throw and catch the Frisbee thirty times just as fast as they can. There should be no more than five teams playing at one time. One judge is needed.

• The game is set up the same as Marathon—teams of two players each, standing facing each other fifteen yards apart, and about five yards away from the next team. The judge calls out the starting time so all players will begin to throw at the same time.

• The team member who throws first calls out the number of each throw—1-2-3-4-5—and so on, until thirty.

• If either partner drops or misses the Frisbee, he or she can step over the throwing line to pick it up, if necessary. But the player must go back behind the line to throw again.

• The first team which finishes the thirty throws and catches is the winner.

During these contests you might find out that you have some pretty good players in your school. How about challenging another school to a tournament? Your school's Frisbee-ers against theirs!

Play your best. But if you lose, don't let it get you down. Remember, Frisbee is for *fun!*

Monika Lou, distance champion, making a spectacular catch

Tournaments and Champs

For Frisbee players, tournaments are not just a place to compete with other Frisbee players. They are a chance to make new friends, to exchange news, and to see champions in action. There are tournaments all over the country almost all year around. Some players cross the country, "traveling the tournament trail."

The first tournament was organized in 1958 in the little northern Michigan town of Escanaba. Actually, it wasn't "organized." It just grew. It started as a Fourth of July picnic where the Healy family and their neighbors got together to throw their Frisbees around. As the years went on, more and more people showed up to join in the fun. The location had to be moved several times because they kept running out of room. Now the

Healy Fourth of July picnic is known as the International Frisbee Tournament, and players come to it from all over the world!

Some tournaments are organized by individual Frisbee clubs, some are sponsored—supported—by colleges and universities, others by local businesses, and some by the IFA. Yale, Northwestern, the University of Michigan, Rutgers, Duke, Cornell, and almost one hundred other colleges and universities have regularly scheduled Frisbee tournaments. Maplewood, New Jersey, had the first high school varsity Frisbee team in the country. Many high schools now have teams.

Fred Lemke, California Junior Champion, under 11 age group, 1976

The United States is not the only country which has Frisbee tournaments. The Canadian Open Frisbee Championships is held every August in Toronto. Germany and South Africa already have junior and senior championships, and many other countries are currently becoming involved in serious competition.

No matter where players come from, they can compete because the International Frisbee Association, organized in 1967, has certain rules and standards. The IFA set up four different classes of Frisbee skill: novice, expert, master, world class master. To advance to the higher classes, each player has to take a test of skill in throws and catches.

Players take these tests in their own town or city so long as they have a judge to watch and keep score. However, the IFA thought it would be a good idea to get together in one place to take some of the tests. So, in 1968, the first International Masters Qualifications Meet was held at the Rose Bowl in Pasadena, California.

It worked out so well that it is a yearly event, and the high point of tournament play.

There are over 72,000 members in the IFA. Members range in age from children who have just barely started to walk to a man in his nineties. And don't leave out the dogs! The IFA has its own K-9 Corps with 1,000 members.

You can join the IFA even if you don't know much about Frisbee playing. All that is required is that you want to know more about the sport.

If you want to join, write to:

The IFA
P.O. Box 664
Alhambra, CA 91802

Send $3.00 with a letter, saying that you would like to have a lifetime membership in the IFA. The IFA will send you a membership card and a proficiency (skills) manual, or booklet. The manual will tell you how to become a Frisbee expert, and how to advance from one rating to another.

The IFA also publishes a magazine, *Frisbee World,* to which you can subscribe.

If you are at least eight years old and not over fifteen, you have your own special Frisbee tournament. The International Junior Tournament was started in 1969. The national finals that year were held in Madison Square Garden (an indoor stadium) in New York City. Since then, almost two million boys and girls have competed in city, state, regional, and national contests, trying to become the International Junior Champion of Frisbee. This competition now has more people in it every year than the Soap Box Derby and the Punt, Pass, and Kick competition combined!

There are no entrance fees to get into the Juniors. All you need is your Frisbee and your IFA membership card. The crown is well worth trying for. The regional winners get free trips to the Nationals. The top players at the Nationals get prizes such as medals, and United States savings bonds. They also appear in the playoffs on a nationally broadcast television show.

Sound good? Then call your local park or recreation department and ask them when a Frisbee competition will be held near your home. 728 communities all over the United States hold these competitions, and the winners are sent to one of nine regional finals. All costs are paid for by the community park and recreation departments, and the Wham-O company. All they want *you* to do is to join the competitions.

And don't be nervous. "If you become tense," says Vic Malafronte, "take a few breaths and loosen your muscles by shaking your arms and fingers."

Jo Cahow believes that it is important to get into as many contests as you can. "But it's not the winning that's important," she says. "Join in even if you don't think you have a chance of winning. You don't have to be the best, but the more you play and the more people you meet, the more self-confidence you are going to have. And the idea is not to just be a better Frisbee player, but a better person."

To give you an idea of what a Junior competition is like, here is a list of things which you will be asked to try.

1. Two accuracy flights through a hula hoop target.
2. Backhand, sidearm, or underhand straight flight into a 12-foot circle to a catcher.
3. Right curve into the circle.
4. Left curve into the circle.
5. Backhand, sidearm, or underhand skipshot into the circle.

6. Behind-the-back catch with either hand.
7. Between-the-legs catch with either hand.
8. A distance flight using a backhand, sidearm, or underhand.

The 1976 Junior National winners were Krae Van Sickle of New York, Chris Johnson of California, and Peter Ronquillo of New Mexico.

Irv Lander is the director of the Junior competitions. He invites *you* to try out.

"Don't hesitate to join whatever Frisbee activity is going on in your community. In Frisbee you don't have to compete with anyone but yourself. One of the best things about good Frisbee players of all ages is that instead of trying to beat out the beginners, they give them a helping hand. People may be strangers when they come to the regionals, but by the time it's over they are all friends. Frisbee is a sport of brotherhood and sisterhood."

Frisbee-ing with Fido

Vic Malafronte, John Kirkland, Jo Cahow, Monika Lou, Mark Stoolz: all Frisbee champions.

Ashley Whippet, Hyper Hank, Bismarck, Schatzie, Martha: they're Frisbee champions, too.

It doesn't matter that only a few of them can throw a Frisbee, and the only kind of catch they can do is with the mouth. Champs they definitely are. They are all *Frisbee dogs!*

In 1974 one hundred of these talented animals showed their Frisbee proficiency at the first annual Fearless Fido Frisbee Fetching Fracas. That event was held in Fullerton, California and the winners were Hyper

Hank, an Australian Shepherd, and Schatzie, a half-huskie, half-shepherd. All of the contestants were given the chance to catch five throws which had been tossed by their owners. They were judged on the average distance for the five catches, plus their style and artistry of movement.

Dogs are an important part of the Rose Bowl Frisbee Championships. In 1974, Bismarck was declared the distance champion, and Ashley Whippet won the altitude competition with his nine-foot leaps into the air.

A spectacular leap by Ashley Whippet

Ashley has appeared on television on the Mike Douglas and the Johnny Carson shows. Mr. Douglas bet Bobby Riggs, who is a famous tennis player, that Mr. Riggs couldn't catch a Frisbee with his mouth as well as a mysterious guest who was waiting behind the curtain. Of course, no one except Mr. Douglas knew that the other guest was a dog.

Yes, Mr. Riggs lost the bet and Ashley became more famous than ever.

Ashley has also played Frisbee at half time at football games and often receives more applause than some of the champion football players.

Hyper Hank has made many television commercials for dog food and peanut butter and for the Wham-O Company. His intelligence has amazed many people.

"Hyper Hank figures out flight trajectories—paths—faster than NASA Control at Houston," says Irv Lander.

Hyper Hank makes a catch

A good Frisbee dog is a joy to watch: leaping, twisting, bounding, sprinting down the field, figuring out just the right time and the right place to catch the Frisbee in midair. Then with a quick snap of the neck, some of the more talented ones toss the Frisbee back toward the owner.

Do you have a dog? If you don't, maybe one of your friends does. Many dogs can be trained to play Frisbee. You may know a future four-footed Frisbee champion.

There are some things to think about before you buy a Frisbee for a dog. Breeds with long noses such as shepherds or Labradors have a better chance to catch flying discs than snub-nosed dogs such as English bulldogs or Pekinese. Besides having such short snouts, these two don't have the breath control and endurance that many other dogs have.

Quickness and agility are important also. Whippets and Setters are usually nimble-footed and enthusiastic Frisbee players.

The "jowly" dogs, whose cheeks seem to hang down over their jaws, often don't do well at the sport. Two examples are the Bassett hound and the bloodhound. These sad-faced dogs are more the type which would love to see *you* chasing the disc. It's as if they were thinking, "Wear yourself out if you want. I'd just as soon not get involved."

Make sure your pet is in good physical condition before you start doing any training. Even then, don't over-do. Many dogs enjoy playing Frisbee so much that they don't know when to stop. When you are tired

you know you should rest. A dog might not be that smart. You will get more done with your dog in many short training sessions than in a few long ones.

Make sure there is water available for your pet. Dogs "dry out" much faster than you do. It is also a good idea to take some honey along, especially on hot days. Give your dog a couple of licks to help replace the energy used in chasing the Frisbee.

Your dog should have his own Frisbee, and while you're at it get one or two extra. A dog's teeth go through Frisbees fast, and jagged plastic edges can cut.

If your dog is small or medium (up to 20 inches at the shoulder) get a Regular Frisbee. For a large dog (20 to 28 inches) a Pro model will be just about right.

Is your dog larger than that? You'd better stock up on Master Frisbees—and stay out of the way when he's chasing one of them!

Let your dog get used to the Frisbee gradually. Let him smell it, lick it, chew on it. If he takes it in his mouth, praise him and pet him to let him know he's getting the idea.

What? He's not interested? Try feeding him his supper in the Frisbee. If there are other Frisbee dogs nearby, put his leash on and take him to see them. No one you know has a Frisbee dog? Then let your dog watch you and a friend throw the Frisbee back and forth. *That* should put some ideas into his head.

When your dog starts to grab hold of the Frisbee without coaxing, you can take the other side and play tug of war. Throw some rollers, and when the dog goes after the Frisbee, let him know he's done something special.

Now that you've aroused your dog's interest in the disc, you can start actual training. Hold the Frisbee in front of you, high up over the dog's head. Then walk backwards calling his name and saying "Jump." When he goes after the Frisbee put it into his mouth. Repeat this over and over until he jumps whenever you hold the Frisbee up.

Now you can try throwing some short flights. Get his attention, throw the Frisbee, and say "Jump." If he has learned the last lesson thoroughly, he should begin chasing the Frisbee. Then your flights can become longer and longer.

If there is one word that's more important than any other in training a dog, that word is *patience.* Be prepared to do the same step over and over again, and be ready for days when there just doesn't seem to be any progress. Your dog really wants to please you. Time and plenty of pats on the head should do it.

You can use bits of a favorite food as a reward after a good lesson. Soon, just catching the Frisbee will be reward enough for him. Your problem may well be getting your dog to stop playing!

When you're playing Frisbee with your dog, it's twice as important to follow the safety rules. Remember, you're watching out for *both* your pet and yourself. Play in an open space. Don't ever throw your dog's Frisbee into the street. Excited, the dog might not look for cars. Make him rest when he gets tired, and give him enough water and food. If he doesn't seem to feel well, don't let him play.

It's *not* a good idea to play Frisbee with two dogs at the same time. They can be thinking so hard about catching the disc that they could run into each other. Bismarck and Ashley Whippet collided with each other one time as they were dashing onto the field. Luckily, they were only stunned. A good Frisbee dog can run at tremendous speeds—fifty miles an hour at times! Hitting something at that speed can mean a bad injury.

You are smart enough to know that no sport—even Frisbee—is worth that.

Good luck to you and your dog. If you both play Frisbee, who knows? One of you might get written up in *Frisbee World!*

Glossary

Air current—a moving stream of air
Air pressure—the push or thrust of air against an object
Air resistance—also called *drag*—the opposition of the air to any object moving through it. This slows the object. You can feel air resistance when you are walking into a strong wind.
Arc—the curved path of your Frisbee through the air
Axis—a straight line passing through the center of an object around which that object turns or revolves. This line can be real or imaginary. The earth's axis is an example of an imaginary axis.
Cheek—the inside surface of the rim of the Frisbee
Cupola—the center of the Frisbee
Density—heaviness or thickness
Downdraft—an unexpected downward thrust of air
Downwind—the same direction the wind is blowing
Eddy—a circular current of air which runs against the main current
Follow-through—Letting the arm finish its swing after throwing
Force—any push or pull on an object
Free-style—throwing, tossing, jumping, catching, running with the Frisbee. "Doing your own thing."
Gravity—the force or "pull" from the earth which draws things toward it
Gust—a short puff of wind, usually lasting only a few seconds
Leading edge—the edge of the Frisbee facing away from the thrower and toward the catcher or target—opposite of trailing edge
Lift—the rising of the Frisbee in the air
Lip—the outside surface of the rim of the Frisbee
Lock—to stiffen or tighten, as at the elbow or wrist
Point of release—the exact time and place at which the Frisbee leaves your hand

Ratio—the balance or proportion between things or numbers. If there are 30 boys in a class and 15 girls, the ratio of boys to girls is 2 to 1, found by dividing 15 into 30.

Spin—the twirling action of the Frisbee

Stability—steadiness

Throwing arm—the arm you throw the Frisbee with

Throwing side—the side of your body that your throwing arm is on

Tilt—slanting the Frisbee to right or left as you hold it

Trailing edge—the side of the Frisbee facing toward the thrower and away from the catcher or target.—opposite of leading edge

Turbulence—when the speed and direction of the wind change often and without warning

UFO—unidentified flying object

Uncock—to loosen your wrist and bend it quickly back with a snap as you let the Frisbee go

Uncurl—to gradually bend your wrist away from your body as you throw the Frisbee

Upwind—the opposite direction to which the wind is blowing—opposite of downwind

Vacuum—a space where there is no air

Velocity—speed plus direction

MEN

Event	Score	Where and When Set	Current Record Holder	From Where
Outdoor Distance	412 ft.	Boston MA 7-24-76	Dave Johnson	Ocean Bluffs MA
Indoor Distance	277 ft.	Los Angeles CA 8-23-75	Dave Johnson	Ocean Bluffs MA
Maximum Time Aloft	15 sec.	Toronto, Canada 8-6-75	Ken Westerfield	Toronto, Ontario, Canada
Throw, Run, & Catch	234 ft.	Boulder CO 7-17-76	John Kirkland	Allston MA
Accuracy	20 of 28	Minneapolis MN 7-10-76	Dan Roddick	Pasadena CA

WOMEN

Event	Score	Where and When Set	Current Record Holder	From Where
Outdoor Distance	283 ft. 6 in.	Boston MA 7-24-76	Susanne Lempert	New York
Indoor Distance	209 ft.	Los Angeles CA 8-23-75	Monika Lou	Berkeley CA
Maximum Time Aloft	9.9 sec.	Los Angeles CA 8-7-76	Monika Lou	Berkeley CA
Throw, Run, & Catch	143 ft.	Santa Barbara CA 3-13-76	Monika Lou	Berkeley CA
Accuracy	15 of 28	Florence AL 6-12-76	Monika Lou	Berkeley CA

JUNIORS (12-16)

Event	Score	Where and When Set	Current Record Holder	From Where
Distance	279 ft.	New York NY June, 1976	Krae Van Sickle	New York NY
Maximum Time Aloft	10.8 sec.	Toronto, Ontario Canada 8-7-76	Krae Van Sickle	New York NY
Throw, Run, & Catch	169 ft.	Los Angeles CA 8-26-76	Krae Van Sickle	New York NY
Accuracy	17 of 28	New York NY June, 1976	Bruce Tashoff	New York NY

CHILDREN (UNDER 12)

Event	Score	Where and When Set	Current Record Holder	From Where
Distance	201 ft.	La Canada CA Jan. 3, 1976	Scott Mc Glasson	Monrovia CA
Maximum Time Aloft	5.7 sec.	La Canada CA Jan. 3, 1976	Scott Mc Glasson	Monrovia CA
Throw, Run, & Catch	84 ft. 6 in.	La Canada CA Jan. 3, 1976	Bobby Stanislaus	Monrovia CA

Index